Windward

A poetry collection

by Stephen Mason

Windward
By Stephen Mason

© 2016 Stephen Mason

ISBN: 9780993526589

Published in 2016 by Arkbound Ltd (Publishers)

No part of this publication may be reproduced, stored in a retrieval system, or transmitted, in any form or by any means without the prior permission of the publisher, nor be otherwise circulated in any form of binding or cover other than that in which it is published and without a similar condition being imposed on the subsequent purchaser.

■■

Arkbound is a social enterprise that aims to promote social inclusion, community development and artistic talent. It sponsors publications by disadvantaged authors and covers issues that engage wider social concerns.

Arkbound fully embraces sustainability and environmental protection. It endeavours to use material that is renewable, recyclable or sourced from sustainable forest.

Arkbound
Backfields House
Upper York Street
Bristol BS2 8QJ
England

www.arkbound.com

This book is dedicated to those who fall, but rise up stronger; to those who see light in the deepest darkest; to those who love and still find wonder in nature, to all who suffer, but don't lose hope.

Foreword to the first edition

This book spans a period of 9 years. The poems follow lose threads of hope, loss, redemption, discovery and courage. They are woven together by a belief in the power of writing, and a continuing faith that humanity can still do immense good as well as harm.

If all us were able to pause and contemplate the world, without prejudice or preconception, we may well be a step closer to paradise. These poems attempt to convey and encourage that sentiment – not as a sermon, but as a developing pathway.

I spent time in the darkest dungeons, walking corridors of despair and longing that I shiver to recall, and one thing that kept holding me up was the belief in a light. Sometimes distant, sometimes cold and indecipherable, but it was always there. Fate, Purpose, God – call it what you will. A fragment of this light lies within each of our hearts, no matter where we have come from or what we have done.

Reach out, find it, and let your light shine.

- SM, East Devon, August

Contents

I

Bluebells	4
Surfing	5
September Night Storm	6
The Crab	7
Musing	8
Monday Night Storm	9
Lost and Found	10
A Butterfly	11
A Rainbow	12
Untitled Unknown	13
Istanbul	14
Green	15
'Bury Wood	16
Never Reaching The End	17

II

The Bonding	21
Remembrances	22
FATE	23
Momento	24
A Prophecy	25
Writing	26
Windward	27

II

Modernity	30
Slow Time	31
The 19th	32
The Salcombe Three	33
The Sun Always Shines	35
The Waste	36
Winter's Renewal	39
ZEBRA	40
Venus	41
Contemplations of Eternity	42

IV

Prometheus Creed	45
26	46
CHARIOT BATTLE	47
Citizens and Slaves	48
Midnight Runners	50
Ode to the Sea Behind Bars	51
WORLD WARRIORS	52

Stephen Mason

I

To dream dreams undreamt of before

Let it be known that the greatest things in life are known through the smallest. A raindrop, a bluebell, a second - each inseparable from the interplay of Being that spans all scales.

My name could be your name. My art could be your own. Can you write the first letter of your calling? Can you paint a mountain stream? It matters not. Writing this, reading this, we have entered the same world. Like the atoms of our molecular makeup, the stardust of blood and bone, the thoughts that weave two concepts together - we have become as one.

There is a land where all is at peace; where the nights are cool and the days are bright. Rolling green hills recede to a tree-lined horizon. Ocean spray dances before sierra-hued cliffs. A crystal stream can be found running in each valley, tracing the fleeting patterns of leaping fish. Bird song clothes the sequinned mist of every amber dawn. Ten million stars play amidst a glittering deck of owl hoots and moonlight.

Behold this beautiful land, for it is before you. On a field, picture the grass move in circulating patterns, bending down to a southwards breeze. See how each green splinter is pressed to its neighbour, separate and yet part of the whole. Feel the air move through your hair, sweeping across your brow. Does it smell of spring or summer? For here there is no long winter, no barren waste of shivering cold.

As shadows race across the grass, skylarks pursue the clouds. They sing a symphony to every facet of creation, like free spirits before the fall. And so, with face uplifted to the infinite sky, towards the azure-veiled heavens, you lose all worries and cares. Even thought is given away to the bliss of being in the present. You lie down on the grass, feeling its springy embrace envelop your body.

Warmed by new sunlight, you float into dreams....

The Bluebells

Under the swirling patterns of sunlight,
Shining through a canopy of trees,
A sea of violet blossoms bloomed:
A dancing host of bells washed blue,
Emerging from bubbling whirlpools
Of different-shaded greens,
Bowing in the buzzing air
With the life of the pollen seeking bees -
Bursting forth, reaching up,
In and out of sunrays.

Freshly a breeze blows through the wood
Carrying spring-time scents
As sparse leaves of last autumn
Twirl in patches of shade,
Crumbling slowly in a world
Which will always be re-made.

From emerald tower to emerald tower
Leaped the squirrels and birds
And oft, with playful pose uplifted,
They seemed to freeze in time
And thrust upon one's beating heart
A living energy sublime.

To see the forest spread
With purple robes of royalty
Finer than the drapery
Of any King or Queen;
The bluebells pledged, through the green,
To God unending loyalty -
Bringing colour, magic, life,
To live in memory eternal.

Surfing

Surfing the waves,
No cares for the world,
In the light, in the water,
In the curving caress
Of Neptune's daughter.

Around about the swirling depths
That reach untouched to places dark -
Unto twilight crystal, lit by turquoise blue,
Amidst a true reclining view.

To reach! And see all horizons
Stretched from point to point:
Rising...
Retreating...
...Creating
Destroying...

In thunderous power unrolling
Each foaming crest
A launch pad into liberty -
Where all is moving
Yet at rest.

September Night Storm

To the stroboscopic horizon my eyes were drawn
Magnetised by the ongoing display of light:
Electric blues, fused into flame,
A blackness shattered by white.

Raindrops metamorphosing
Into ever-widening pools -
A power too great to contemplate,
Plunging down from ozone falls,
Drawing the energies of Earth and Sky,
Constructing a masterpiece
Unmatched by any hand or eye.

Before the mighty thunderheads,
Flashing with frothing fury,
I stood before each shaking crash -
Brow beaten, ears lashed.

Zenith high those skies did break!
Ruled by whatever clouds could create -
Bullets of gold shattering sand,
A quivering gloss of glory.

It passed, it passed,
Perhaps too soon -
Beating out a final rhythm
Like the march of a hero's platoon,
Into the distance...
Into the ever-dying dark...
Trembling.

The Crab

The Crab crawled to St. Austell
Crossing a tundra of sand
Claws tracing lines that withered
To the sea's unfurling band;
Playing on, playing on, wave
On wave touching coloured grains
Whilst Crab carried on from its cave.

Finding safety behind a solitary stone,
Stalk-eyes scanning bird-bombarding skies,
Onwards that crazy Crab did roam
Like some battle-wearied knight
In rainbow-streaked armour
As passing children ran in fright
To the sight of its claws in the harbour.

But crawl no longer it did
As one bold gull swooped down,
Reversing Crab's carcass like a lid
And pecking, pecking -
Eating a second or third tea,
Then dropping Crab's carcass
                        Beneath the sea.

Musings

On Earth, just look and wonder, see
or remember...

The peace of a summer's eve,
Where swallows trace the last sunrays,
And crickets lift a song to the rising stars
As shadows lengthen, bringing colour in contrasts;
A hinge upon the splendour of dawn and dusk,
Rising as one sets...

Behold the valleys of spring, so green!
Where trees unfurl their new-found canopies
As birds declare their crafted homes,
Singing with a wind's gentler sigh;
Behold the river flowing, gushing forth!
Like life's very essence
Sparkling in moonlight, a gemstone bridge,
Floating on aerial vapours,
As of snowdrops coated in pearl;
The thoughts of reclaimed destiny
Become what was...

And what will be.

Monday Night Storm

Every echo, reaching from hill to hill,
Sending waves through ripples;
With each flash, objects leap forth
In unpredictable relief,
Becoming known from nothing,
Darkness surrendering to light.

Fleetingly another reminder
Of impermanence;
Long shadows of self but projections
Of conceptions;
A web of silver strings
Hung upon life's fibre -
One raindrop changes it all.

Round upon elements cycling,
Oceans of Being re-forming,
Aspirations receding like pebbles
In backwashed tides, drawn behind inexorably
To a mirror of limitless expanse.

Slowly the storm of emotion quietens,
Thunder clouds giving way
To rays of sunlight, like arrows
In a blue sky beyond.

Form is emptiness
And emptiness also is form -
One giving rise to another,
Waves from ever-present winds,
Slowly shaping continents
As continents are moved by the world.

Lost and Found

The sound of waves on the shore,
The sight of moonlight on the Severn
As swans glide by,
The smell of wild garlic
By the shady forest stream,
The touch of a summer breeze
And feel of misty morning dew,
The taste of a crisp apple from a tree,
The knowledge that tomorrow
Is whatever you make of it,
That horizons are never set.

Mountains capped with ice,
Oceans rolling turquoise plumes,
Meadows of green, rushing streams,
The cool breeze on a starlit spring night,
Grass vales sparkling with dew,
Wild wind-swept plains of running horses,
The shade of palm trees or oaks
Cast by summer sun,
Long lost footprints on golden-pressed sand,
Winter snow on a frozen morning,
Autumn colours from fallen leaves,
Being at peace, content and happy -
This is freedom.

A Butterfly

A butterfly floats above a brook,
Slowly ascending it dances on air,
Its image reflected in fleeting water,
Facets of wings and jewel-like eyes
Dance upon every surface
Like sapphires entrapped by amber.

Only shadows stir beneath the trees,
A windless symphony
Up-taking a silent song,
As, with turquoise flight rotating
The winged-wonder up-rises,
Chasing rays of light
Like threads of dreams.

A Rainbow

Rain, Sun, Mist -
Drops of life alighting on green,
Rays of colour splintered off sand,
Veils of white floating round hills;
Together, spreading rainbows,
Building dream worlds in life's big dream.

Making contours in vapour,
Paths through the boughs of trees,
Valleys between ocean waves -
Softly, softly floats the ashes of yesterday
Ever-reforming into motion.

Sunrays glance off broken roofs,
Forgotten mirages of lost dreams
Echoing like leaves drifting
On an aimless breeze.

Two turquoise butterflies dance
Above a crystal rushing stream;
Twisting, intertwining
In double-helix patterns,
Tracing the essence of all life.

Never a stone remains
Nor tide un-turning;
In endless cycles the world unravels
Like a magic origami model.

Untitled Unknown

To dream dreams undreamt before,
To crest gold waves unfurling,
Thundering down a forgotten shore -
Reach high, reach high
To a naked sky,
With leaden arms outstretched,
Like a phoenix, fly!

Look aloft to sapphire gems,
Their sequinned reams outspread;
Dwell not on transient trends,
Darkened by envy and spite -
See above and around,
Across mountains clothed in might,
Where wind gusts build a sound
More like a song -
Something *here*, embracing hopes,
Then flowing on...

A key to fit time's fated contour
Like a cloud creased on a vanquished decree
To set a night's sun free
To solve the puzzle upon life's door:-
'What Is,
Will Be.'

Istanbul

Glowing minarets reach as pinnacles
To a moonlit, untouched sky;
Silver rays flood fountains
Washing the city walls dry...

Seagulls drift betwixt the towers
Like ghosts bound by memories
Of the muezzin's calls,
Joining shadows
That fall in the catacombs below...

In some ways unchanged
Since Caesars trailed robes before armies
And sultans sat before councils of the wise,
When cities were seen as the second prize
And the world itself the first...

Days long gone, long forgotten,
Yet still drawing motion
In Constantinople's silent mirages.

Stephen Mason

Green

Uplifting green, renewing green
All around the emerald colours glow
In light and shade, oscillating
In spiralling patterns of growth -
Moss green on fallen branches,
Ivy green on upright trees,
Bright sunlit leaf green!
The green of carpeted bluebells -
Every breath a taste of life.

A gust blows, caught on aerial
Drifts of chaos, yet every breeze
Brings mambas to oak leaves,
Turning forest branches to sylvan triangles,
Which tinkle in uncountable sounds,
Foretelling a song unknown -
Above, below, beyond,
Nature's spring garment
Spread in joy.

'Bury Wood

Golden sunrays spread a haze
In the sylvan-emerald maze;
Amidst violet robes, a blue bell flotilla
Bloomed beneath the outspread bough's.

Bees buzzed through light and shade
Like nymphs afloat in magic air -
A kingdom created, not made,
Enough to cast away all worry and care.

On the softly woven ground I stood,
Green it was, and vibrant hues un-weaved
Scattered ways in circles
Like of a sacred tapestry.

Catching my ears and thoughts, songs
Of blackbirds, thrushes, sparrows,
Voices of squirrels emerging from burrows,
Flashing red-tinted tails from branch to branch.

Indeed it was some kind of dance
Not just betwixt the swaying bough's
But through the host of flowers,
Spread beneath those leaning towers.

A thousand scents came on a breeze
Awaking the founding of spring,
And no glistening crown or royal robe
Could match this living majesty.

I gazed and gazed, in unfolding bliss -
To look upon a sight so bright
And be lifted, high into blue
Like a bird, soaring, I flew.

Never Reaching The End

All night we lay under a thousand stars;
Knights rode on silver clouds
Across a crescent moon;
Waves rolled in, one by one,
Caressing the sands;
A turquoise touch to cool our hearts aflame,
Our sighs mixed with the wind's
Soulful whisper;
Our heartbeat,
One.

II

Knowing God's right hand

Listen unto this symphony and behold a marvel. See the heights of cresting splendour, feel the gusts from Neptune's realm, hail the blithe spirits of another age! For 'tis the ghosts of vanquished time that call with such sagacious doom, foretelling what is yet to be. Can a skeletal finger weave a cloak of silk, spinning a pattern that no eyes see? Shall we cast our bets on the die of fortune, hoping for the right set of dots? Think not how their surfaces tumble; dwell not on the obtuse angles - the path is set, the landing unavoidable.

Ah lo! That such a meeting would always be bound, etched into some golden ring like runes of necromancy - a spell that can never, not ever, be broken.

Utter the Word, whisper it with fear (and perhaps an iota of repressed loathing); that Word which pounds its force upon the Earth, like Thor's thundering hammer and the Sky Lord's brand, frozen into bone and soil with each burning impartation:-

Fate.

I say it again: Fate.

Trembling, quivering with its very quivers, we cannot escape the Right Hand of Mighty God. He dwells with and beyond the very stars, encircling planets with His Breath, reaching from the furthest void to the hidden worlds beneath mortal sight. Light, bright and beautiful, as mysterious and incomprehensible as the very darkness it conquers, is only a shadow of His Being. That the most wondrous thing in all creation - the painter of form, of colour, of life itself - should be but a faint sketch of His Presence...

Light is the shadow of God, as a grey stone is a shadow of the blasting energy of its atoms; as a bird carries with it the infinite beauty of the sky.

The Bonding

Over the sprinkled embers
of forgotten morrows
a glow that floats anew
rises up to warm us.

As sunrays melt the snow
feeding rivers, filling lakes,
so does your breath
break the fear of loss.

On a night wrapped in moonrays
your voice floats through the mist -
a butterfly that sits on drunken lips
quivering in timeless beauty.

Whisper, my love, of eternity;
touch me, oh goddess
and set this moment in gold;
to chase away the dark
and live within a heartbeat.

Remembrances

Golden roofed temples uprising above dusty streets,
Trails of saffron-robed monks walking in line,
Stone faces of forgotten gods
Poised on the pinnacles of Jungle ruins,
Gazing into a windy infinity.

Elephants trudging towards the sun,
Bats curving over rocky hills,
Dolphins leaping from turquoise surf,
Gargoyle crocodiles lazing on mangrove sand.

Cities of countless cathedrals,
Skyscrapers glistening in splendour
Red to the blood they shed.

The pine grove before the mountain,
The red cliffs before a crashing sea,
A stream meandering through a valley,
Sand rolled endlessly into dunes.

Deep, deep blue harbouring miracles of colour,
A night sky to capture a millennia's dreams,
The drop of dew upon the grass blade,
A beginning and an end.

FATE

To change one's Fate
Is that the greatest Feat?
Of all the many paths
Not one fails to meet.

Is this road already set,
Laid stone by tragic stone?
With each falling footstep
Are we destined to walk alone?

From dawn's gate
To destiny's causeway,
Fate overshadows all -
From humanities slow rise
To its eventual, apocalyptic Fall.

No hand can change the course
Except the one unseen -
We are all energy-atoms
Caught in time's eternal force.

Momento

Some days are alike to a glistening crescent moon
Trapped in an ebony ocean and gone too soon;
Some hours seem to flee
When the heart is filled with glee,
Whilst others crawl along like snails,
So ponderously slow,
When everything to hope for
Is but a distant glow
And the seconds - so quickly they pass
Like uncountable sand grains
Trapped in an hour glass
Or as raindrops frozen into snow -
No two alike, upon the winds they blow;
Caught on the currents and threads of Fate
And before dream's are made real, it's too late.
But Lo! To stand upon a peak
Or look down into a precipice
Finding you're unable to speak
Fixed in a moment of endless bliss
Like two lovers in their first kiss
Or the artist's rapture sublime,
Sketching fragments of future 'morrows,
Perhaps to touch the unpainted divine.
In such time there is no hour or second -
Only the present to beckon,
To banish both future and past.

A Prophecy

When the Earth is split by man-made borders
And every country, ocean and shore is mapped;
When no uncharted lands remain,
Or final frontiers to wander;
When roads outnumber rivers
And cities outnumber mounts
Then the ground will groan
And the skies will tremble -
Only the stars, or annihilation,
Will be our legacy.

Writing

O beautiful lines
that bridge the contours of Being
they weave a cloak
across my weather-beaten frame
Yes, O Muse
who surpasses all barriers
who knows the signs
You breath a hope and glory
onto every creation;
a boat, a bridge, a wing,
to make the vital connection.

Windward

The wind blows strong
Through the trees it rushes on
Over hilltops unwinding
Singing out a rhythmic song
Where magic and mystery still belong.

To pause and catch a whisper
Riding high on Earth's breath;
Sweeping in aerial ribbons,
Chasing the sunrays and shadows
Behind life's invisible thread.

Can you feel it a'blowing?
Deep throbbing as arterial blood
Within and without, ever-flowing
Like a thought that falls abridge of Time -
Ungrasped, unbounded.

It's written on the water
Golden fields flashing blue
Deep as winter nights, whirled
In satin resplendence -
Running on,
Running on...

III

See the shadows moving in the silence

Can one stand in the midst of an acrid waste and walk away pure? Can one traverse a territory of darkness without being blinded by the return of light? Is it possible to regain what has so hopelessly been destroyed, lost, and half-forgotten?

For that is the virtue of adversity: it can destroy, and it can also re-create. One can fall and stay fallen, or rise up stronger. It all depends on one's disposition.

Modernity

Behold this ruined land
of shattered dreams and quartered hopes
strewn with ash and embers.
Statues of forgotten art
lie smashed and broken;
the pillars of righteous courts
are fallen, buried - to ashes
all has gone.

Even frogs ford rivers
and crocodiles befriend birds -
so unlike the human race,
bestowing one inch of light
for every acre of darkness,
one fingertip of warmth
for the press of frozen limbs,
one smile
out of every thousandth frown.

Yet hoping, in phantom scrawl to change,
with every etch to make a better world,
tracing fate's contours like waves,
smoothing a jagged, unforgiving shore
and dying out at birth.

Slow Time

Twilight over the emerald eaves,
A gradual shift of hues from green to grey,
A final burst of colour - then darkness.

Days go on like rivers flowing,
Nights pass like clouds floating,
Past and future untouched, illusory,
Like the shimmering of a desert mirage.

Count the seconds and hours
And slow will the sands move on,
Creeping will the crashing waves unfurl,
Like a snail cresting a mountain;
But sit upon the rock, and gaze
Upon a moonlit lake -
Light from one surface to another,
Reflecting in quiet contemplation,
Then there is no time to count.

The 19th

Fates of uproarious spoil
Sweeping down with sharpened claws,
In stabbing ascendance uplifting
Across mighty cities, barren lands,
Over mountains, through clouds,
Until -
Betwixt the dangling teeth of death -
Dropped down, no longer flying,
In merciless descent disappearing
From every ray of warmth and light;
Into darkness dwelling,
Into anger igniting -
Becoming but a wraith, enslaved by metal;
A ring that binds both hand and heart,
Ruined in a cycle of voided abandon.
Where, o where, the way of hope?
When, o when, the time of dreams?
'Tis gone beyond the dungeon doors,
Deep as a sunken ship,
Distant as a sparkling star,
Gone with all things green and good,
As - lost - I wander in the shade.

Stephen Mason

The Salcombe Three

A choice to die,
a vow to live,
upon the cliff three hearts
decided.

Gazing, hands clasped, across
a tapestry of light and water,
wondering, perhaps, what
would happen next.

Death's obsidian unknown
promises only endings
but for them
that was enough.

...

I passed the place at night
drawn by moonlight dreams
to gaze, like them, across
the sighing south-east horizon;

Hearing, so gently, a calling,
a fragment of another's thought,
freezing me with awe:
a promise the pain would be over,
an urge to take the same plunge,
dying young and living free.

One step, one choice,
simplicity corroded to resolve -
I turned away and fled,
too scared to look behind,
too sorry to remember.

...

But still, after trekking a road
paved with pain and sorrows,
I wish, sometimes,
I joined them.

The Sun Always Shines

How did it come to be -
A bright world of colour
Cast into darkness
With the drifting of shadowy night?
Running water no longer sparkling,
Vibrant greens no longer a'flower,
Even the songs of birds are silenced.

But under thick mammatus domes
Beneath foreboding flashes,
From cumuli-nimbus walls,
A thought passes, so silently:
'The sun always shines,
Although it is hidden
By clouds sometimes.'

And like a raindrop falling,
Like a crashing wave unfurling,
Swift passes the dark,
Disappearing to a reign of light,
Colours return - birdsong resounds -
Life's treasure, once more, restored.

The Waste

Sun's auroral glow
Shatters quartered dreams
What can one day bestow
But hopes torn at the seams?

Bare be the flakes
In diversity descending,
A mountain crescending,
Coating rivers in pearl
But none are falling
In this hell.

Razor-set steel
Peaked to snag an innocent sky
With amber clouds streaked
Too chalky to cry.

What wounded waste
Could match that saddened vault
Where sun and moon give chase?
Stars sprinkled salt
Answer no anguished imploration,
Always silent
To every shout of desperation.

Another year
To pierce the fear
And one thought alone proclaims:
"It will not,
It cannot,
End here."

A token as-yet unbroken,
Planted on an unploughed land,
Like some footprint slowly fading,
Eroding on the burning sand.

Torment

Watching gluttony as you starve;
Seeing the fire consume what you newly carved;
Hearing laughter as you weep in deepest despair;
Casting a friendship beyond all hope of repair;
Watching lovers as you walk alone,
No stolen soul mate can safely atone;
Hearing birds sing behind the jail cell walls;
Unable to get up, even after countless falls.

Touching a sunray in a collapsed cave;
Growing old, watching life seasonally re-made;
Getting a drop of water in the desert, but not a glass;
Being too late for the first class;
Forgetting the lines of a favourite song;
Winning a lottery, then finding your wrong.

Alas, for torments come and go
But you should think hard and know:
For every hell, a glimmer of paradise gains -
In the mind, over clouds, in the darkness
A shining light remains.

Winter's Renewal

Simmering flotillas of decaying leaves
Descending on dying air
No longer binded by the trees
To feel the springtime sun.

They rest upon a carpet
Patterned by lost sierra
No longer touched by summer rays
Which sparkled on still water.

Just to lie.
And rot.

Worms trace the veins
Of each skeletal carcass
Into the soil eroding
From cavernous unknowns uprising
To brighten the green of future renewal.

ZEBRA

Zebra flying high
        high like grass in summer
nip-nipping over hills, over there
        right here
wobbling up a dune
        rolling , rolling
                in savannah shade.
Zebra going home
Zebra striped no longer,
        Legs a-strumming rhythmic beats
        a plain already set
                kindled by Ra.
                      Sierra she-tiger leaps
unknown
                      Roars and slashes wild
        fighting, kicking, dying,
        the Zebra -
                food.

Stephen Mason

Venus

Volcanic planet, 2nd from the sun, 'the morning star'

Orb of the eastern horizon,
Morning star of coldest nights,
Brightest point outshining all others -
On a lake in a mountainous land,
I see you smile;
Through the forest arches,
You lead the way;
Across the arid dunes,
The journey's guide.

World where imagination
Bloomed new paradise:
Flowing streams, mist-clothed valleys,
Flowers and plants growing bright.
From such a veil of unknown,
In the heart of your being,
Is it possible to find such wrath?

Blazing heat that tore the chance of life away
Vaporizing the essence, blasting
Away all hope.
Too close to the furnace,
And too far away to know
In your brightness, only illusions were born.

Contemplations of Eternity

Whiskey would not go amiss -
A bottle, a glass, a dram,
One final lick of fire
And then... and then...

Tumbling down
Down. down, down
You never see the ground
Not even when it hits you.

One cloud, floating
In one great unending sky,
Its home could be forever
As its kingdom is the start.

Amber drops are falling
Against a jealous bloody sun
Maybe painted, maybe sketched,
With not a hand to frame 'em.

I see an eye
That shimmers in silver,
An echo of the past
And when I blink... no longer.

IV

Hear the captain's courage in the singing wind

For all man's evil, for every bloody battle and darkest deed, there are flashes of light. Speckled through the wretched annals of history, they shine like something out of a dream – unbreakable, unassailable and pure. They are not shrouded in abstract concepts but built from common blood and bone.

From the protector of innocents to the rebel against tyranny; from the liberator of slaves to the defender of cities, we look across time and find them standing. Courageous, strong, alone - they are the world's warriors. Within us all their Will can pulse, reaching out to be heard, ever waiting for the chance to redeem and to strengthen.

Prometheus Creed

As blood drips from platinum clouds,
as darkness dips its beak into my heart,
a constant swirl of loss and ignorance and fear
wraps around this platform of surrender.
To die, to live, to never rise again,
and still the winds of change whisper,
still a life of dead tomorrows
crumbles over sand;
a sand that weeps with every wave -
to dust it goes, in ground it sinks,
like a bead that breaks from its chain,
trampled by a blind-folded crowd,
its pieces split and crushed,
stamped into oblivion.
But Lo!
A diamond heart remains unconquered
In adversity's vice it only grows strong;
no glass bead is this, no little trinket -
this sparkling fire within my breast:
the Strength to Fight, to forge through darkness,
to become what all hearts should be,
beating in synchrony with another
                right to the shores of infinity.

26

26 years and much I've seen,
26 years and much I've been,
But of this quarter century
More sorrow than gladness has come my way,
More tears than laughter, more loss than gain;
For mistakes made, I've been forced to pay
And my dreams lie soaked in blood, slain
By the dark mechanisms of a relentless system.

Fallen in the shadows of a rotten state
An ember remains to rise, reaching
For a rising renewal -
As old as I am, as young as I was
To go on:
To keep on fighting,
To know what is right,
To treasure day and night,
To value nature and life,
To make new dreams, and share them
In love, and together to last forever
As one with the changing world.

CHARIOT BATTLE

Chariots of fire, careering towards the embankment,
Blasting, splintering spears of oblivion,
Towards the seething shields the wheels turn on,
Throwing up clouds of dust and smoke,
Ascending higher those plumes up-rise.

> Slowly, gradually, swings the formation,
> Glittering clearly to an unremitting sun,
> Mirror-like metal polished to perfection,
> Javelin spears thrust forth, edges locked,
> To that great wheeled sea the wall stands.

Trumpets blaring notes of courage,
Wheels still rolling, colours flying,
Proud flags fluttering,
Arrows unleashed, raining death -
Falling armour, broken limbs,
Blood stains the soil a brighter brown.

> Row upon row of shields stand yet,
> The chariot charge clashes like thunder
> Against a mighty cliff -
> But swings away, defeated.

Citizens and Slaves

There was an anarchist's rose,
Trampled on stone,
Bled across city spires -
Their goals set not by dreams
But by artificial ambition.

A name and a number,
Coded and filed,
To each assigned,
Carefully classified,
Facelessly defined.

You're a commodity
Taught to consume,
To be kept closely, gripped tightly -
Blood for the oil of economy,
Flesh for a trigger,
Bone for bricks.

Instructed to obey,
Punished to question
A law never signed,
A tax never brokered,
Like orders and tithes
Called down from above -
"Do that. Pay this.
Or else!"

No movement
Without consent,

Stephen Mason

No settlement
Without citizenship -
What are borders
But bars of a bigger cage?

An anarchist rose
Branded from birth,
Red on the streets -
Knowing the State is the slaver
And the citizen is the serf.

Midnight Runners

Midnight runners to a moonlit sky,
        every eye
a mirror to countless suns,
sparkling in lustrous serenades.

Gently, gently
their fleeting song up-rises,
slowly it falls
like ice-rimmed leaves:-

"Red, red, the rivers flowing...
O to taste
        a drop,
to sit unburned in sunshine...
onwards through towns that die
        tomorrow.
Life's stream flows on,
but on to where?"

Heaven and earth alike resound
to every frozen syllable
yet every word
remains unheard.

No shadows run beside them,
no lovers live to walk away;
only a swirl of fallen tears
tells of their crimson passage.

Onwards they run
endlessly out-chasing sunrays,
wind-skimmed skin like ivory,
                  racing till the dawn.

Stephen Mason

Ode to the Sea Behind Bars

As the sun shines outside and a warm wind blows,
Scented with the green growth of late July,
I think of you, your cooling touch -
A cleansing wash to gladded the spirit;
Your waters ever moving to moon and stars,
Sparkling to the rays of dawn,
Blazing to the red of sunsets;
A thousand gems interlacing from diamond white,
Splintering into lapis lazuli and turquoise sapphire
Then falling into caverns of amethyst fire.

As deep as your depths, my heart aches for you,
Where life in all its majesty arose and formed;
Where animals drift in your currents
From rainbow fishes to huge blue whales;
Where coral forests of colour bloom in shallow warmth;
Where mists clothes you by the coasts at morning.

Rising waves of splendour breaking upon gusts of wind,
Storms to tear the strongest rocks asunder,
And yet a peace, a presence, so silent and great
Lies throughout you, like an aura
That comes to light upon the world,
Bringing life.

WORLD WARRIORS

When the burnished bronze
Of vanquished armies
Corrodes to bloody sand
And every polished sword
Lies split and broken...
When the hero has fallen
And the general is gone
There remains, like a star,
The will to fight again.

Can you glimpse a knight's chivalry
In the unfurling blade of grass?
Can you hear the captain's courage
In the singing wind?
A storm declares its wrath,
The sea its vastness,
The sky its dreams,
And each, together,
                Does battle with time.